To:

From:

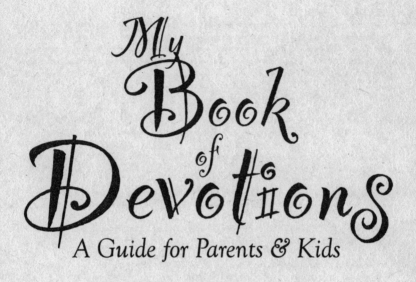

My Book of Devotions

A Guide for Parents & Kids

about Sharing

Simon & Schuster, Inc.

NEW YORK LONDON TORONTO SYDNEY

Simon & Schuster, Inc.
1230 Avenue of the Americas, New York, New York 10020

Cover Design by Kim Russell / Wahoo Designs
Page Layout by Bart Dawson

Manufactured in the United States of America

10 9 8 7 6 5 4 3 2 1

ISBN-13: 978-1-4169-1595-9
ISBN-10: 1-4169-1595-8

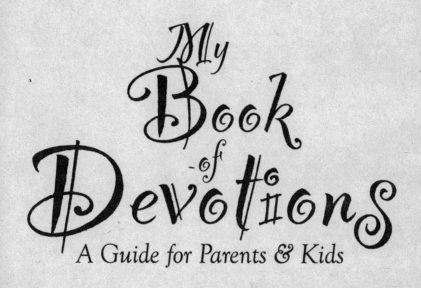

My Book of Devotions

A Guide for Parents & Kids

about Sharing

Always try to do
what is good
for each other
and for all people.

1 Thessalonians 5:15 ICB

Table of Contents

A Message for Parents

The fact that you've picked up this book means that you're a concerned, thoughtful parent—congratulations. When you spend time reading to your youngster, you're helping your child build a strong intellectual and spiritual foundation.

This little book—which is intended to be read by Christian parents to their young children—contains 31 brief chapters, one for each day of the month. Each chapter consists of a Bible verse, a brief story or lesson, kid-friendly quotations from notable Christian thinkers, a tip, and a prayer. Every chapter examines a different aspect of an important Biblical theme: sharing.

For the next 31 days, take the time to read one chapter each night to your child, and then spend a few moments talking about the chapter's meaning. By the end of the month, you will have had 31 different opportunities to share God's wisdom with your son or daughter, and that's good.

If you have been touched by God's love and His grace, then you know the joy that He has brought into your own life. Now it's your turn to share His message with the boy or girl whom He has entrusted to your care. Happy reading! And may God richly bless you and your family now and forever.

Kindness Starts with You!

We must not become tired of doing good.
We will receive our harvest of eternal life
at the right time if we do not give up.

Galatians 6:9 NCV

Day 1

If you're waiting for other people to be nice to you before you're nice to them, you've got it backwards. Kindness starts with you! You see, you can never control what other people will say or do, but you can control your own behavior.

The Bible tells us that we should never stop doing good deeds as long as we live. Kindness is God's way, and it should be our way, too. Starting now!

Big Idea for Kids

Kindness every day: Kindness should be part of our lives every day, not just on the days when we feel good. Don't try to be kind some of the time, and don't try to be kind to some of the people you know. Instead, try to be kind all of the time, and to all of the people you know.

When you extend hospitality to others,
you're not trying to impress people,
you're trying to reflect God to them.

Max Lucado

Big Idea for Parents

Want them to know what Jesus would do? Then teach them what Jesus did!

Today's Prayer

Dear Lord, help me to remember
that it is always my job to treat
others with kindness and respect.
Make the Golden Rule my rule,
and make Your Word my guidebook
for the way I treat other people.
Amen

Sharing Is God's Way

If you have two shirts, share with
the person who does not have one.
If you have food, share that too.

Luke 3:11 ICB

Day 2

You've heard it plenty of times from your parents and teachers: share your things. But it's important to realize that sharing isn't just something that grown-ups want you to do. It's also something that God wants you to do.

The word "possessions" is another way of describing the stuff that belongs to you: your clothes, your toys, your books, and things like that are "your possessions."

Jesus says that you should learn how to share your possessions without feeling bad about it. Sometimes, of course, it's very hard to share and very easy to be stingy. But God wants you to share—and to keep sharing! Since that's what God wants, it's what you should want, too.

Big Idea for Kids

What does the Bible say about sharing our possessions? The Bible answers this question very clearly: when other people need our help, we should gladly share the things we have.

How generous you are does not depend
on how much you give,
but how much you have left.

Anonymous

Big Idea for Parents

Toy referees of the world, unite: It's almost Biblical: when two or more small children are gathered together, they are bound to fuss over toys. Use these disagreements as opportunities to preach the gospel of sharing (even if your sermon falls upon inattentive little ears!).

Today's Prayer

Dear Lord, I know there is
no happiness in keeping Your blessings
for myself. Today, I will share
my blessings with my family,
with my friends, and people
who need my help.
Amen

Helping People Who Need It

The one who blesses others is
abundantly blessed;
those who help others are helped.
Proverbs 11:25 MSG

Day 3

Lots of people in the world aren't as fortunate as you are. Some of these folks live in faraway places, and that makes it harder to help them. But other people who need your help are living very near you.

Ask your parents to help you find ways to do something nice for folks who need it. And don't forget that everybody needs love, kindness, and respect, so you should always be ready to share those things, too.

Big Idea for Kids

Where can you share? Look around. Soon, you'll have a chance to share a helping hand or a kind word. So keep your eyes open for friends who need your help, whether at home, at church, or at school.

> We hurt people by being too busy,
> too busy to notice their needs.
> Billy Graham

Big Idea for Parents

Preach, teach, and reach . . . out!: When it comes to teaching our children about helping others, our sermons are not as important as our service. Charity should start at home—with parents—and work its way down the family tree from there.

Today's Prayer

Dear Lord, let me help others
in every way that I can.
Jesus served others; I can too.
Today, I will share my possessions
and my prayers. And, I will share
kind words with my family
and my friends.
Amen

The Rule That's Golden

Do for other people the same things
you want them to do for you.
Matthew 7:12 ICB

Day 4

Do you want other people to share with you? Of course you do. And that's why you should share with them. The words of Matthew 7:12 remind us that, as believers in Christ, we should treat others as we wish to be treated. And that means that we should share our things with others.

The Golden Rule is your tool for deciding how you will treat other people. When you use the Golden Rule as your guide for living, your words and your actions will be pleasing to other people and to God.

Big Idea for Kids

How would you feel? When you're trying to decide how to treat another person, ask yourself this question: "How would I feel if somebody treated me that way?" Then, treat the other person the way that you would want to be treated.

> Make the most of today.
> Translate your good intentions
> into actual good deeds.
>
> Grenville Kleiser

Big Idea for Parents

The Golden Rule in Action! When you live according to the principle of the Golden Rule, your children will notice, and the results will be as good as gold . . . make that better than gold!

Today's Prayer

Dear Lord, help me always to do
my very best to treat others as
I wish to be treated.
The Golden Rule is Your rule, Father;
let me also make it mine.
Amen

What the Bible Says

Your word is a lamp to my feet
and a light for my path.
Psalm 119:105 NIV

Day 5

What book contains everything that God has to say about sharing? The Bible, of course. If you read the Bible every day, you'll soon be convinced that sharing is very important to God. And, since sharing is important to God, it should be important to you, too.

The Bible is the most important book you'll ever own. It's God's Holy Word. Read it every day, and follow its instructions. If you do, you'll be safe now and forever.

Big Idea for Kids

Read the Bible? Every Day! Try to read your Bible with your parents every day. If they forget, remind them!

The Bible is the treasure map that leads us to God's highest treasure: eternal life.

Max Lucado

Big Idea for Parents

It's up to us: Our children will learn about Jesus at church and, in some cases, at school. But, the ultimate responsibility for religious teachings should never be delegated to institutions outside the home. As parents, we must teach our children about the love and grace of Jesus Christ by our words and by our actions.

Today's Prayer

Dear Lord, the Bible is Your gift
to me. I will use it, I will trust it,
and I will obey it, today
and every day that I live.
Amen

It Comes from the Heart

Every way of a man is right in his own eyes,
but the Lord weighs the hearts.
Proverbs 21:2 NKJV

Day 6

Other people see you from the outside. God sees you from the inside—God sees your heart.

Kindness comes from the heart. So does sharing. So if you want to show your family and your friends that your heart is filled with kindness and love, one way to do it is by sharing. But don't worry about trying to show God what kind of person you are. He already knows your heart, and He loves you more than you can imagine.

Big Idea for Kids

Talk about your feelings: If something is bothering you, tell your parents. Don't be afraid to talk about your feelings. Your mom and dad love you, and they can help you. So whatever "it" is, talk about it . . . with your parents!

It is the thoughts and intents of
the heart that shape a person's life.
John Eldredge

Big Idea for Parents

Be Expressive: Make certain that at your house love is expressed and demonstrated many times each day. Little acts of consideration and kindness can make a big difference in the way that your child views the world.

Today's Prayer

Dear Lord, thank You for loving me.
I will return Your love by sharing it
. . . today and every day.
Amen

The Things You Don't Need

Trust in your money and down you go!
But the godly flourish like leaves in spring.
Proverbs 11:28 NLT

Day 7

Do you have more toys than you can play with? Do you have clothes that you no longer like to wear? If so, it's time to start thinking about who could use them.

Talk to your parents about ways to share the things you aren't using. Remember this: somebody out there would gladly use these things; in fact, somebody out there needs these things. And it's up to you and your parents to find that somebody—and share.

Big Idea for Kids

Finding loving homes for clothes and toys: your parents can help you find younger children who need the clothes and toys that you've outgrown.

> The more we stuff ourselves
> with material pleasures,
> the less we seem to appreciate life.
> Barbara Johnson

Big Idea for Parents

A system of family values that is built upon the Rock: It's up to you to insure that your family's value system is built on the Rock that cannot be moved. As a parent, you must help your children understand that obeying God's Word is a priority that never comes "next."

Today's Prayer

Dear Lord, help me to be a kind
and generous person.
The Bible tells me to share my things.
I won't wait to share them;
I will share them now.
Amen

Sharing with Family

The first thing they need to learn is
to do their duty to their own family.
When they do this, they will be
repaying their parents or grandparents.
That pleases God.

1 Timothy 5:4 ICB

Day 8

A good place to start sharing is at home—but it isn't always an easy place to start. Sometimes, especially when we're tired or mad, we don't treat our family members as nicely as we should. And that's too bad!

Do you have brothers and sisters? Or cousins? If so, you're lucky.

Sharing your things—without whining or complaining—is a wonderful way to show your family that you love them. So the next time a brother or sister or cousin asks to borrow something, say "yes" without getting mad. It's a great way to say, "I love you."

Big Idea for Kids

Since you love your family . . . let them know it by the things you say and the things you do. And, never take your family members for granted; they deserve your very best treatment!

There is so much compassion and understanding that is gained when we've experienced God's grace firsthand within our own families.

Lisa Whelchel

Big Idea for Parents

As Children Grow Older, Give Them Age-appropriate Responsibilities: Household chores can be wonderful teaching tools. Employ them.

Today's Prayer

Dear Lord, You have given me a family
that cares for me and loves me.
Thank You. I will let my family know
that I love them by the things that
I say and do. You know that
I love my family, Lord.
Now it's my turn to show them!
Amen

Sharing with Friends

A friend loves you all the time,
and a brother helps in time of trouble.
Proverbs 17:17 NCV

Day 9

How can you be a good friend? One way is by sharing. And here are some of the things you can share: smiles, kind words, pats on the back, your toys, school supplies, books, and, of course, your prayers.

Would you like to make your friends happy? And would you like to make yourself happy at the same time? Here's how: treat your friends like you want to be treated. That means obeying the Golden Rule, which, of course, means sharing. In fact, the more you share, the better friend you'll be.

Big Idea for Kids

You make friends by being a friend. And when you choose your friends, choose wisely.

The best times in life are made
a thousand times better when shared
with a dear friend.
Luci Swindoll

Big Idea for Parents

Before your child's friends come over for a visit: remind your child that he or she is the host, and that sharing with guests is an important way to demonstrate hospitality.

Today's Prayer

Dear Lord, thank You for my friends.
Let me be a good friend to other
people, and let me show them what
it means to be a good Christian.
Amen

The Time to Share Is Now!

Always try to do what is good
for each other and for all people.
1 Thessalonians 5:15 ICB

Day 10

When is the best time to share? Whenever you can—and that means right now, if possible. When you start thinking about the things you can share, you probably think mostly about things that belong to you (like toys or clothes), but there are many more things you can share (like love, kindness, encouragement, and prayers). That means you have the opportunity to share something with somebody almost any time you want. And that's exactly what God wants you to do—so start sharing now and don't ever stop.

Big Idea for Kids

How about sharing a hug right now? The person who's reading you this book deserves one!

Nothing is really ours until we share it.
C. S. Lewis

Big Idea for Parents

The importance of "now": as a parent, you know that procrastination is an easy habit to acquire and a difficult habit to break. When the time is right, help your child learn the value of self-discipline and the importance of doing first things first.

Today's Prayer

Dear Lord, there are so many things
that I can share. Help me never
to forget the importance of sharing
my possessions, my prayers,
and my love with family members
and friends.
Amen

It's Tempting to be Selfish

Don't be selfish; don't live to make
a good impression on others.
Philippians 2:3 NLT

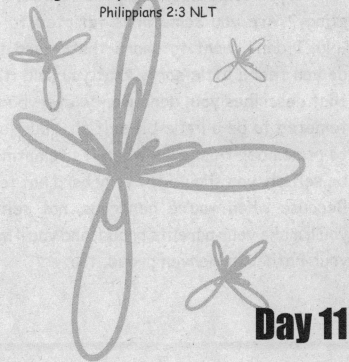

Day 11

It's tempting to be selfish, but it's wrong. It's tempting to want to keep everything for yourself, but it's better to share. It's tempting to say, "No, that's MINE!" but it's better to say, "I'll share it with you."

Are you sometimes tempted to be a little stingy? Are you sometimes tempted to say, "No, I don't' want to share that!"—and then do you feel a little sorry that you said it? If that describes you, don't worry: everybody is tempted to be a little bit selfish. Your job is to remember this: even when it's tempting to be selfish, you should try very hard not to be. Because when you're generous, not selfish, you'll make your parents proud, and you'll make your Father in Heaven proud, too.

Big Idea for Kids

Tempted to get into an argument? Walk away. The best fights are those that never happen.

To show great love for God and our neighbor, we need not do great things. It is how much love we put in the doing that makes our offering something beautiful for God.

Mother Teresa

Big Idea for Parents

When it comes to courteous behavior, you're the most important role model: so pay careful attention to the way that you treat other people, especially those who are not in a position to help you. For further instructions, read Matthew 25:40.

Today's Prayer

Dear Lord, Your Son Jesus was
never selfish. Let me follow in
His footsteps by sharing with
those who need my help.
Amen

Helping Others Is Fun

Happy is the person who . . .
loves what the Lord commands.

Psalm 112:1 ICB

Day 12

Helping other people can be fun! When you help others, you feel better about yourself. And, you know that God approves of what you're doing.

When you learn how to cooperate with your family and friends, you'll soon discover that it's more fun when everybody works together. And one way that you can all work together is by sharing.

So do yourself a favor: learn better ways to share and to cooperate. It's the right thing to do, and besides: it's more fun.

Big Idea for Kids

Do you need a little cheering up? Cheer up somebody else. When you brighten somebody else's day, you brighten up your own day, too.

Do all the good you can. In all the ways
you can. In all the places you can.
At all the times you can. To all the people
you can. As long as you can.
John Wesley

Big Idea for Parents

Sharing every day . . . Each day offers countless opportunities to share. Seize these opportunities. When you do, you'll help your child understand that sharing should be woven into the fabric of everyday events.

Today's Prayer

Dear Lord, Your love is so wonderful
that I can't really imagine it,
but I can share it . . . and I will . . .
today and every day.
Amen

Let Your Light Shine

You are the light that gives light to
the world. In the same way, you should be
a light for other people. Live so that
they will see the good things you do
and will praise your Father in heaven.
Matthew 5:14,16 NCV

The Bible says that you are "the light that gives light to the world." The Bible also says that you should live in a way that lets other people understand what it means to be a good person. And, of course, learning to share is an important part of being a good person.

What kind of "light" have you been giving off? Hopefully, you have been a good example for everybody to see. Why? Because the world needs all the light it can get, and that includes your light, too!

Big Idea for Kids

Let your light shine by being respectful: Everybody is important to God. And you should treat every person with courtesy, dignity, and respect.

> It is a great deal better to live
> a holy life than to talk about it.
> Lighthouses do not ring bells,
> they just shine.
> D. L Moody

Big Idea for Parents

Live According to the Principles You Teach: The sermons you live are far more important than the sermons you preach.

Today's Prayer

Dear Lord, let my light shine brightly for You. Let me be a good example for all to see, and let me share love and kindness with my family and friends, today and every day.

Amen

The Good Samaritan

Then a Samaritan traveling down
the road came to where the hurt man was.
When he saw the man, he felt very sorry
for him. The Samaritan went to him,
poured olive oil and wine on his wounds,
and bandaged them. Then he put the hurt
man on his own donkey and took him to
an inn where he cared for him.
Luke 10:33-34 NCV

Day 14

Sometimes we would like to help make the world a happier place, but we're not sure how to do it. Jesus told the story of the "Good Samaritan," a man who helped a fellow traveler when no one else would. We, too, should be good Samaritans when we find people who need our help.

So what can you do to make God's world a better place? You can start by making your own corner of the world a little nicer place to live (by sharing kind words and good deeds). And then, you can take your concerns to God in prayer. Whether you've offered a helping hand or a heartfelt prayer, you've done a lot.

Big Idea for Kids

Does a friend or family member need your help? Then be a Good Samaritan by sharing a helping hand, a friendly word, or a happy smile.

We ought not to be weary of doing little things for the love of God, who regards not the greatness of the work, but the love with which it is performed.

Brother Lawrence

Big Idea for Parents

Good Samaritan 101: You're the teacher. Class is in session. Your child is in attendance. Actions speak louder than words. And it's one of the most important courses you will ever teach.

Today's Prayer

Dear Lord, when my family or friends need me, let me behave myself like the Good Samaritan. Let me be helpful, generous, and kind . . . today, tomorrow, and every day of my life.

Amen

Pray About It!

Make this your common practice:
Confess your sins to each other and pray
for each other so that you can live together
whole and healed. The prayer of a person
living right with God is something
powerful to be reckoned with.

James 5:16 MSG

Day 15

If you are upset, pray about it. If you're having trouble sharing, ask God to help you. If there is person you don't like, pray for a forgiving heart. If there is something you're worried about, ask God to comfort you.

As you pray more and more, you'll discover that God is always near and that He's always ready to hear from you. So don't worry about things; pray about them. God is waiting . . . and listening!

Big Idea for Kids

Open-eyed prayers: When you are praying, your eyes don't always have to be closed. Of course, it's good to close your eyes and bow your head, but you can also offer a quick prayer to God with your eyes open. That means that you can pray just about any time.

> Prayer connects us with
> God's limitless potential.
> Henry Blackaby

Big Idea for Parents

Don't Ever be Embarrassed to Pray: Are you embarrassed to bow your head in a restaurant? Don't be; it's the people who don't pray in restaurants who should be embarrassed!

Today's Prayer

Dear Lord, help me remember
the importance of prayer.
You always hear my prayers, God;
let me always pray them!
Amen

Learning to Share

Assuredly, I say to you,
inasmuch as you did it to one of
the least of these My brethren,
you did it to Me.
Matthew 25:40 NKJV

Day 16

If you're having a little trouble learning how to share your stuff, you're not alone! Most people have problems letting go of things, so don't be discouraged. Just remember that learning to share requires practice and lots of it. The more you share—and the more you learn how good it feels to share—the sooner you'll be able to please God with the generosity and love that flow from your heart.

Big Idea for Kids

Practice, Practice, Practice: Want to get good at sharing? Start by sharing little things, and work your way up from there.

Some people give time, some give money,
some their skills and connections,
some literally give their life's blood.
But everyone has something to give.
Barbara Bush

Big Idea for Parents

Parental demonstrations on the art of sharing: Your children will learn how to treat others by watching you (not by listening to you!). Your acts of kindness and generosity will speak far louder than words.

Today's Prayer

Dear Lord, help me to learn
the importance of sharing.
The Bible teaches me to share,
and so do my parents. Now, it's up
to me to learn how to share the things
that I have—and it's up to me to
share kind words and good deeds
with my family and friends.
Amen

You'll Feel Better About Yourself

So think clearly and exercise self-control.
Look forward to the special blessings
that will come to you at the return
of Jesus Christ.
1 Peter 1:13 NLT

Day 17

The more you share, the quicker you'll discover this fact: Good things happen to people (like you) who are kind enough to share the blessings that God has given them.

Sharing makes you feel better about yourself. Whether you're at home or at school, remember that the best rewards go to the kids who are kind and generous—not to the people who are unkind or stingy. So do what's right: share. You'll feel lots better about yourself when you do.

Big Idea for Kids

Feeling better about yourself by helping other people: When talking to other people, ask yourself this question: "How helpful can I be?" When you help others, you'll be proud of yourself, and God will be, too!

The way you see yourself and the world has a whole lot to do with how happy you are.

Zig Ziglar

Big Idea for Parents

Feeling good about yourself as a parent: The perfect parent does not exist. So don't be too hard on yourself when you fall short of absolute perfection (or, for that matter, when you fall short of near perfection). Do your best, and trust God with the rest.

Today's Prayer

Dear Lord, help me to slow down
and to think about my behavior.
And then, help me to do the right
thing, so that I can feel better
about myself . . . and You can, too.
Amen

God Knows

I am the Lord, and I can look
into a person's heart.
Jeremiah 17:10 ICB

Day 18

Even when nobody else is watching, God is. Nothing that we say or do escapes the watchful eye of our Father in Heaven.

God understands that we are not perfect, but even though He knows that we make mistakes, He still wants us to live according to His rules, not our own.

The next time that you're tempted to say something that you shouldn't say or to do something that you shouldn't do, remember that you can't keep secrets from God. So don't even try!

Big Idea for Kids

Big, bigger, and very big plans. God has very big plans in store for you, so trust Him, and do your best to obey His rules.

God is at work; He is in full control;
He is in the midst of whatever has happened,
is happening, and will happen.

Charles Swindoll

Big Idea for Parents

Jesus loves you, this you know . . . and they should, too! Of course you know that Jesus loves you. But it's up to you to make sure that they know that you know. So remind them often.

Today's Prayer

Dear Lord, You know my heart.
And, You have given me a conscience
that tells me what is right and what
is wrong. I will listen to that
quiet voice so I can do the right thing
today and every day.
Amen

Be a Good Example

In everything set them an example
by doing what is good.
Titus 2:7 NIV

Day 19

What kind of example are you? Are you the kind of person who shows other people what it means to share? Hopefully you are that kind of person!!!

Whether you realize it or not, you're an example to your friends and family members. So today, be a good example for others to follow. Because God needs people (like you) who are willing to behave themselves as God intends. And that's exactly the kind of example you should always try to be.

Big Idea for Kids

Your friends are watching: so be the kind of example that God wants you to be—be a good example.

Our walk counts far more than our talk, always!

George Mueller

Big Idea for Parents

Calling all parents! What the world needs is more parents who are willing to be positive role models to their children. God wants you to be that kind of parent . . . now!

Today's Prayer

Lord, make me a good example
to my family and friends.
Let the things that I say and do
show everybody what it means to be
a good person and a good Christian.
Amen

Too Much Stuff

Then Jesus said to them,
"Be careful and guard against all kinds of
greed. A man's life is not measured
by the many things he owns."
Luke 12:15 ICB

Day 20

A re you one of those kids who are lucky enough to have a closet filled up with stuff? If so, it's probably time to share some of it.

When your mom or dad says it's time to clean up your closet and give some things away, don't be sad. Instead of whining, think about all the children who could enjoy the things that you don't use very much. And while you're at it, think about what Jesus might tell you to do if He were here. Jesus would tell you to share generously and cheerfully. And that's exactly what you should do!

Big Idea for Kids

Too many toys? Give them away! Are you one of those lucky kids who have more toys than they can play with? If so, remember that not everyone is so lucky. Ask your parents to help you give some of your toys to children who need them more than you do.

If you want to be truly happy, you won't find it on a never-ending search for more stuff.
Bill Hybels

Big Idea for Parents

As your children grow into adulthood, some of the most precious possessions from their childhood will be memories. So keep lots of photos, notes and cards from friends and family members, and a few treasured keepsakes. Your little angels will grow up sooner than you can imagine. And when they do, one of the great gifts you can give them is a box-full (and a heart-full) of happy memories.

Today's Prayer

Dear Lord, sometimes it's easy to think
only of myself, and not of others.
Help me remember that I should treat
other people in the same way that
I would want to be treated if I were
standing in their shoes. You have
given me many blessings, Lord—
let me share them now.
Amen

The Greatest Teacher

Mary, sat at the Lord's feet,
listening to what he taught.
Luke 10:39 NLT

Day 21

Who was the greatest teacher in the history of the world? Jesus was . . and He still is! Jesus teaches us how to live, how to behave, and how to worship. Now, it's up to each of us, as Christians, to learn the important lessons that Jesus can teach.

Some day soon you will have learned everything that Jesus has to teach you, right? WRONG!!!! Jesus will keep teaching you important lessons throughout your life. And that's good, because all of us, kids and grown-ups alike, have lots to learn . . . especially from the Master . . . and the Master, of course, is Jesus.

Big Idea for Kids

Learning about Jesus: Start learning about Jesus, and keep learning about Him as long as you live. His story never grows old, and His teachings never fail.

We must always invite Jesus to be
the navigator of our plans, desires, wills,
and emotions, for He is the way,
the truth, and the life.
Bill Bright

Big Idea for Parents

Make Christ the cornerstone: Every family is built upon something; let the foundation of your family be the love of God and the salvation of Christ.

Today's Prayer

Dear Lord, You are my Teacher.
Help me to learn from You.
And then, let me show others
what it means to be a kind,
generous, loving Christian.
Amen

When Others Don't Share

I tell you, love your enemies.
Pray for those who hurt you.
If you do this, you will be true sons
of your Father in heaven.
Matthew 6:44-45 ICB

Day 22

Face it: sometimes people aren't nice. And when other people don't share, you may be tempted to strike out in anger. Don't do it! Instead, remember that God corrects other people's behaviors in His own way, and He probably doesn't need your help. And remember that God has commanded you to forgive other people, just as you seek forgiveness from others when you misbehave. So, when other people aren't nice, forgive them as quickly as you can. And leave the rest up to God.

Big Idea for Kids

Count to ten . . . and keep counting: If you're mad at someone, don't say the first thing that comes to your mind and don't strike out in anger. Instead, catch your breath and start counting until you are once again in control of your temper.

A keen sense of humor helps us
to overlook the unbecoming, understand
the unconventional, tolerate the unpleasant,
overcome the unexpected, and
outlast the unbearable.

Billy Graham

Big Idea for Parents

Respect for All People: Children may seek to find humor in the misfortunes of others; children may, on occasion, exhibit cruelty towards other children. Be watchful for such behaviors and correct them with enthusiasm and vigor.

Today's Prayer

Lord, when I become angry, help me
to remember that You offer me peace.
Let me turn to You for wisdom,
for patience, and for the peace
that only You can give.
Amen

It Makes You
a Better Person

Oh, the joys of those who are kind to
the poor. The LORD rescues them
in times of trouble.

Psalm 41:1 NLT

Day 23

It's a fact: sharing makes you a better person. Why? Because when you share, you're doing several things: first, you're obeying God; and, you're making your corner of the world a better place; and you're learning exactly what it feels like to be a generous, loving person.

When you share, you have the fun of knowing that your good deeds are making other people happy. When you share, you're learning how to become a better person. When you share, you're making things better for other people and for yourself. So do the right thing: share!

Big Idea for Kids

Would you like to be a little happier? The Bible says that if you become a more generous person, you'll become a happier person, too.

> Happiness is obedience to God.
> C. H. Spurgeon

Big Idea for Parents

Living your life and shining your light . . . on your children: As a parent, the most important light you shine is the light that your own life shines on the lives of your children. May your light shine brightly, righteously, obediently, and eternally!

Today's Prayer

Dear Lord, I can't really enjoy
my blessings until I share them.
Let me learn to be a generous person,
and let me say "thanks" to You
by sharing some of the gifts
that You have already given me.
Amen

Sometimes Sharing Is Hard

Remember the words of Jesus. He said, "It is more blessed to give than to receive."
Acts 20:35 ICB

Day 24

Jesus said, "It is more blessed to give than to receive." That means that we should be generous with other people—but sometimes we don't feel much like sharing. Instead of sharing the things that we have, we want to keep them all to ourselves. That's when we must remember that God doesn't want selfishness to rule our hearts; He wants us to be generous.

Are you lucky enough to have nice things? If so, God's instructions are clear: you must share your blessings with others. And that's exactly the way it should be. After all, think how generous God has been with you.

Big Idea for Kids

Kindness every day: Kindness should be part of our lives every day, not just on the days when we feel good. Don't try to be kind some of the time, and don't try to be kind to some of the people you know. Instead, try to be kind all of the time, and try to be kind to all of the people you know.

There is no happiness in having,
or in getting, but only in giving.
Henry Drummond

Big Idea for Parents

Talk about it: If you child seems to be having trouble sharing, don't hesitate to talk things over with your youngster. The more you talk about sharing, the more likely your child is to share.

Today's Prayer

Dear Lord, it's easy to share with some people and difficult to share with others. Let me be kind to all people so that I might follow in the footsteps of Your Son.

Amen

Sharing Cheerfully

God loves a cheerful giver.
2 Corinthians 9:7 NIV

Day 25

How many times have you heard someone say, "Don't touch that; it's mine!" If you're like most of us, you've heard those words many times, and you may have even said them yourself.

The Bible tells us that it's better for us to share things than it is to keep them all to ourselves. And the Bible also tells us that when we share, it's best to do so cheerfully. So today and every day, let's share. It's the best way because it's God's way.

Big Idea for Kids

When am I old enough to start giving? If you're old enough to understand these words, you're old enough to start giving to your church and to those who are less fortunate than you. If you're not sure about the best way to do it, ask your parents!

When we bring sunshine into the lives
of others, we're warmed by it ourselves.
When we spill a little happiness,
it splashes on us.
Barbara Johnson

Big Idea for Parents

Cheerful generosity is contagious: kids catch it from their parents.

Today's Prayer

Dear Lord, help me be a generous
and cheerful person. Let me be kind
to those who need my smile,
and let me share with those
who need my help, today
and every day.

Amen

Too Young to Share?

You are young, but do not let anyone treat you as if you were not important.

1 Timothy 4:12 ICB

Day 26

How old should you be before you should start learning how to share your stuff? If you're old enough to understand these words (and you are!), then you're plenty old enough to learn how to become a person who cooperates and shares.

Have you noticed that small babies aren't very good at sharing? No wonder! They're too young to know better—but you're not. So do what you know is right: share!

Big Idea for Kids

With more birthdays comes better behavior: as you grow up, you'll keep learning better ways to behave yourself. The more candles on your birthday cake, the better you'll be expected to behave—and the easier it will become to behave yourself.

> The maturity of a Christian
> cannot be reached in a moment.
> All of us are growing up in Christ.
> Hannah Whitall Smith

Big Idea for Parents

Age level and maturity level matter: Be sure that the expectations you hold for your child are appropriate for his or her stage of development. As the old saying goes: "kids will be kids." And as a responsible parent, you should let your kid be one, too.

Today's Prayer

Dear Lord, while I am growing up,
I still have so many things to learn.
Let me remember that the most
important lessons are the ones
that I learn every day from
my parents and from You.
Amen

Sharing with Your Church

For we are God's fellow workers;
you are God's field, you are God's building.
1 Corinthians 3:9 NKJV

Day 27

When the offering plate passes by, are you old enough to drop anything in it? If you are, congratulations! But if you're not quite old enough to give money to the church, don't worry—there are still lots of things you can share!

Even when you don't have money to share, you still have much to give to your church. What are some things you can share? Well, you can share your smile, your happiness, your laughter, your energy, your cooperation, your prayers, your obedience, your example, and your love.

So don't worry about giving to the church: even if you don't have lots of money, there are still plenty of ways you can give. And the best time to start giving is NOW!

Big Idea for Kids

Got Money? Share It! Have you ever earned money for doing things around the house? Or have you ever received money as a gift? If so, ask your parents to help you decide on the best way to share some of it.

> Joyful living means joyful giving.
> E. Stanley Jones

Big Idea for Parents

Teaching Generosity: It's never too early to emphasize the importance of giving. From the time that a child is old enough to drop a penny into the offering plate, we, as parents, should stress the obligation that we all have to share the blessings that God has shared with us.

Today's Prayer

Dear Lord, thank You for my church.
When I am at church, I will be
generous, kind, well-behaved,
and respectful. And when I am not
at church, I will act the same way.
Amen

Healthy Habits

Do not be misled:
"Bad company corrupts good character."
1 Corinthians 15:33 NIV

Day 28

Our lives are made up of lots and lots of habits. These habits help determine the kind of people we become. If we choose habits that are good, we are happier and healthier. If we choose habits that are bad, then it's too bad for us!

Sharing, like so many other things, is a habit. And it's a habit that is right for you.

Do you want to grow up to become the kind of person that God intends for you to be? Then get into the habit of sharing the gifts that your Heavenly Father has given you. You'll be glad you did . . . and so will God!

Big Idea for Kids

Choose your habits carefully: habits are easier to make than they are to break, so be careful!

You will never change your life until you change something you do daily.

John Maxwell

Big Idea for Parents

The Importance of Having Healthy Habits: the old saying is familiar and true: "First you make your habits; then your habits make you." So it's always a good time to ask this question: "What kind of person are my habits making me?"

Today's Prayer

Dear Lord, help me form good habits.
And let me make a habit of sharing
the things that I own and the love
that I feel in my heart.
Amen

Solomon Says

Here is my final advice:
Honor God and obey his commands.
Ecclesiastes 12:13 ICB

Day 29

Solomon wasn't just a king. He was also a very wise man and a very good writer. He even wrote several books in the Bible! So when He finally put down His pen, what was this wise man's final advice? It's simple: Solomon said: "Honor God and obey His commandments."

The next time you have an important choice to make, ask yourself this: "Am I honoring God and obeying Him? And am I doing what God wants me to do?" If you can answer those questions with a great big "YES," then go ahead. But if you're uncertain if the choice you are about to make is the right one, slow down. Why? Because that's what Solomon says . . . and that's what God says, too!

Big Idea for Kids

Simon says? Solomon says! Have you ever played the game Simon Says? When you play it, you're not supposed to move until the leader calls out, "Simon Says!" Wise King Solomon had many rules for living. You should get to know those rules—especially the ones found in the Book of Proverbs. Then, you can be guided by the things that Solomon says!

God's mark is on everything that obeys Him.
Martin Luther

Big Idea for Parents

Get to know the Book of Proverbs: and help your child get to know it, too (a children's translation of the Bible can help!).

Today's Prayer

Dear Lord, when I play by Your rules,
You give me wonderful rewards.
I will read the Bible, Lord,
so I can learn Your rules—
and I will obey Your rules,
today and always.
Amen

How They Know You're a Christian

My dear, dear friends, if God loved us
like this, we certainly ought to
love each other.
1 John 4:11 MSG

Day 30

How do people know that you're a Christian? Well, you can tell them, of course. And make no mistake about it: talking about your faith in God is a very good thing to do. But telling people about Jesus isn't enough. You should also show people how a Christian (like you) should behave.

God wants you to be loving and giving. That way, when another other person sees how you behave, that person will know what it means to be a good Christian . . . a good Christian like you!

Big Idea for Kids

Christians are . . . kind and respectful: As a Christian, you must make sure that you show proper respect for everyone, even if that person happens to be different from you. It's easy to make fun of people who seem different . . . but it's wrong.

> A person ought to live so that everybody knows he is a Christian.
>
> D. L. Moody

Big Idea for Parents

Be Expressive: Make certain that your own faith in God is expressed and demonstrated many times each day. Frequent expressions of worship and praise will make a big difference in the life of your child.

Today's Prayer

Dear Lord, help me to make
Your world a better place.
I can't fix all the world's troubles,
but I can help make things better
with kind words, good deeds,
and sincere prayers. Let my actions
and my prayers be pleasing to You,
Lord, now and forever.
Amen

What Jesus Shares with You

For God so loved the world that he gave
his only Son, so that everyone who
believes in him will not perish
but have eternal life.

John 3:16 NLT

Day 31

Who's the best friend this world has ever had? Jesus, of course! When you invite Him into your heart, Jesus will be your friend, too . . . your friend forever.

Jesus has offered to share the gifts of everlasting life and everlasting love with the world . . . and with you. If you make mistakes, He'll still be your friend. If you behave badly, He'll still love you. If you feel sorry or sad, He can help you feel better.

Jesus wants you to have a happy, healthy life. He wants you to be generous and kind. He wants you to follow His example. And the rest is up to you. You can do it! And with a friend like Jesus, you will.

Big Idea for Kids

When in doubt, think about Him. When you have an important decision to make, stop for a minute and think about how Jesus would behave if He were in your shoes.

Christ's love is like a river
that never stops flowing.

Jonathan Edwards

Big Idea for Parents

Jesus is the light of the world. As a caring parent, it's up to you to make certain that He's the light of your family, too.

Today's Prayer

Dear Lord, thank You for Your Son.
Jesus loves me and He shares so much
with me. Let me share His love
with others so that through me,
they can understand what
it means to follow Him.
Amen

Bible Verses
to Remember

But when the Holy Spirit has come
upon you, you will receive power
and will tell people about me everywhere—
in Jerusalem, throughout Judea,
in Samaria, and to the ends of the earth.

Acts 1:8 NLT

Mary was sitting at Jesus' feet and listening to him teach.

Luke 10:39 ICB

Teach me Your way, O LORD; I will walk in Your truth.

Psalm 86:11 NASB

I am the Lord, and I can look into a person's heart.

Jeremiah 17:10 ICB

Let your speech be alway with grace . . . .

Colossians 4:6 KJV

When a believing person prays, great things happen.

James 5:16 NCV

Each of us will be rewarded for his own hard work.

1 Corinthians 3:8 TLB

Happy is the person who . . . loves what the Lord commands.

Psalm 112:1 ICB

Do not love the world or the things in the world. If you love the world, the love of the Father is not in you.

1 John 2:15 NCV

Always try to do what is good for each other and for all people.

1 Thessalonians 5:15 ICB

Your heart must not be troubled. Believe in God; believe also in Me.

John 14:1 HCSB

A friend loves you all the time, and a brother helps in time of trouble.

Proverbs 17:17 NCV

God is spirit, and those
who worship him
must worship in spirit
and truth.

John 4:24 NCV

Your word is like a lamp for my feet and a light for my way.

Psalm 119:105 ICB

Blessed are they which do
hunger and thirst after
righteousness:
for they shall be filled.

Matthew 5:6 KJV

If you have two shirts,
share with the person who
does not have one.
If you have food,
share that too.

Luke 3:11 ICB

God loves a cheerful giver.

2 Corinthians 9:7 NIV